Boudoir Photography Guide

A Women's Bible for a Sexy Dramatic Album, Dress in Outfits, Heels,

Corsets, Robes or Underwear

Thanks for reading!

Table of Contents

Introduction:

Photography has changed how we view the world and how we save our memories. Through photos we are able to capture a moment in our lives that can never be recaptured. Boudoir photography has now become one of the ways women capture their bodies in the natural form to create sexy memories of themselves even as they mature with age and go through the various stages in their life. The practice has once again gained increasing popularity from when it was first famous in the 1920s to the 1940s. Though it has become more mainstreamed through the participation of celebrities in this venture on various cover magazines, it has become more popular with other women who want to celebrate the sexy female form.

We all desire to be sexy and to be seen in the light of that sexiness and this book explains how this journey to boudoir photography started, the importance of boudoir and how to successfully pose for boudoir photography. The ideas are endless and the benefits tremendous. As women we have our lives involved in working hard to do things for others and to please others and sometimes forget how important we are and we tend to listen to the inner critic on all the aspects of our lives. The negative voice within that notices our flaws and imperfections can be ignored and we can celebrate how sexy and how beautiful all our imperfections are through the boudoir photography.

Boudoir once a term used to describe a secret place where women would go to dress is now no longer a secret and is now being used to make women feel sexy and confident about their bodies once again. Being sexy shouldn't be downplayed by anyone and no one should put you down about your body. As a woman you need to exude confidence in your daily tasks as it affects you and those around you in a way that can either be positive or negative.

So enjoy learning and book your first boudoir session with ease and with the skills learnt here you will see the sexy woman within.

Chapter 1: The History of Boudoir Photography

The female form has always been seen as a work of art and thus artists have found a way to adore the female body. From centuries ago even before photography was invented boudoir was done using painting. These paintings focused on the unclothed woman and appreciate her curves and nude body. It started with the Ancient Greek who used paintings and sculptures to make the art of boudoir. The naked form has been used to also depict the gods and goddesses in Greek history. Then the athletes and performers in the ancient Greek were also depicted in their nude form. The body was celebrated by artists from that time and the naked form was an interesting piece of artwork.

Boudoir photography became quite popular in the 1920s and the 1940s especially with the actresses of that period from Jane Russell, Marilyn Monroe and Jean Harlow. Boudoir was used in both photography and film. In the early 1900s the naked female form was celebrated in both film and photographs. It started off as nude photography but photographers later started creating glamorous photos of women that were quite tasteful and showed innocence in the photos. People were intrigued with the female body and everyone was doing it without having to worry about size and shape of the body. The people were featured in magazines and it was done tastefully to create an artistic vision.

Somewhere along the line the conservative nature took over and nudity and boudoir was regarded as something that affected the morality of individuals and boudoir took a step back only practiced privately. This shaming of women then led to the creation of the Play Boy Magazine which men had secret copies of and these photos were of nude women.

More recently boudoir has started getting increased popularity with the modern celebrities starting to bare it down for causes. Several actresses, women of influence and models have started doing naked photo shoots in support of breast cancer. Nudists have come to appreciate the art form of the naked body and nude colonies are on the rise. While this book is not asking you to burn all your clothes and run off to join a nude colony it is merely suggesting that the body is something beautiful in whichever form it is in and you should appreciate your body as a work of art. Boudoir photography will help you get rid of the negative criticism from other and from yourself by helping you discover how naturally sexy you are. Once you are able to see yourself as a sexy being you will be able to ignore anyone who would want to put you down especially for how you look. Women who are plus size or who have had babies are nowadays constantly running to the gym the next day after giving birth to get the ideal shape back and with boudoir photography you will be able to love yourself and while you can strive to lose weight and get fit the motivation shouldn't be based on what other people are thinking of you. You can lose the weight at your own time and for your own reasons and not because society has a size zero as the perfect woman.

Other women have started doing boudoir photography to just have a memory of themselves in their current body form. Others are doing it for their significant others as a gift.

Whichever the reason boudoir is the new form of art that will improve your self-confidence by appreciating your entire body with photographs. Then you can get to choose the sort of pictures that you want taken and how you want to be dressed for it. This art even from the past has always encouraged that women be sexy in whatever they wear from negligees to no dressing whatsoever.

Boudoir is now accepted as a sexy way to view yourself and having a professional photographer to take the photos means you can be captured in the best light so you can get to see how beautiful you look without any clothes on. Boudoir photography is not a morality factor and once you get over the conservative approach you will get to see that it is a professional way to photograph your body in a sexy manner without having to lose your dignity while at it.

The female form should still be celebrated because of the many roles a woman has to play in the society and with the increased popularity many more women can learn to appreciate their bodies and to have the strength to stand up to men in whatever they do.

There is a campaign for free the nipple that has encouraged the increase of boudoir photos revealing women's nipples. It was started by Scout Willis to show that just as men can go topless without repercussions women can and should do it too. The campaign has been supported by Miley Cyrus and Chelsea Handler. This campaign has encouraged women to love their own skin and fought for them not to be ostracized for what they wear or don't wear.

This show of history just proves how beautiful the female form is and how through the various years artists are still fascinated and intrigued by it. They want to take photos and to be able to capture the sexiness of women whether for private view or public view. You can now be able to access a boudoir photo studio with ease and get the photographer to take photos of you naturally without any clothes on. Women need to embrace their beauty so they can raise their self-confidence to enable them to feel sexy no matter what size or what type of figure they have.

Chapter 2: Importance of boudoir Photos

Boudoir photography has increased and the reasons for each lady doing are different. One thing that boudoir photos do is improve yourself confidence. It may surprise you to learn that how you see yourself in the mirror is not how the world sees you. Most women look at the mirror and the negative thoughts start streaming in their mind about their size, shape, freckles, cellulite and other body representations that they make them put themselves down. However, when you take boudoir photos you get to see yourself as a sexy and beautiful woman who can actually get with whoever she wants. These photos empower women and help them get rid of the negative image of themselves. One such lady who went through a boudoir photo shoot was Karen Katib from North Yorkshire. Her husband surprised her one day when he told her he had paid for a session for her. At the time she had a 6 month old daughter whom she was breastfeeding and she just felt overweight. After a few weeks she decided to go for it and got to do a pin up photo shoot. When she saw the photos it completely changed her perception towards her body. She now felt confident and sexy and more comfortable with her body.

The boudoir photos have also served to help people begin a new life. Women who have suffered from breast cancer and have had treatments that have gone as far as mastectomy take boudoir photos to give them hope and the strength to go through the process. It helps bring to light their inner sexy diva so they can feel confident enough to overcome anything. Denise Whittingham had just had a mastectomy and had just been diagnosed with terminal cancer and the treatments had even led to the loss of her hair. Her friends booked for her a session so she could celebrate her current health and the pictures helped to raise her self-esteem and her self-worth.

Taking boudoir photos will help you become happier with the person that you are. It helps appreciates your body in its current state. You learn how to love yourself just as you are because the beautiful sexy photos bring out your best features which you might not notice when looking in the mirror.

Basically you can find that you have always been sexy even without the lingerie and the sexy outfits. Taking these photos requires you to have the sexy attitude and not many people can pull it off. Being able to pose sexily and take photos in front of the camera will help you realize how gorgeous you are.

Even when you conduct a quick search on the internet to find boudoir pictures you will find women of all shapes and sizes. This will help you understand why you should love yourself in whatever form you have and in your current body shape. Women go through a lot of trials and often see themselves in a negative light due to society's demand that they be a certain weight and size with a certain figure. This only leads to people eating things they don't like to maintain shape and others even go for plastic surgery to 'correct' how they look. This negative view has women spending a lot of money trying to get rid of wrinkles, stretch marks and scars but boudoir helps a woman love herself in her own skin whichever way she looks. When you start taking your own boudoir photos you will realize how sexy you are and why you shouldn't change a thing about yourself unless you really want to. Women need to stop being stereotyped as to having one figure type because we are all different and the differences are what make us unique and beautiful.

Chapter 3: Types of Boudoir Photography

When you think of boudoir photos the first thing on your mind may be nude photos or just some cheap porn looking photos but this is not the case. Boudoir photos are a beautiful representation of the female body. They are done with perfect lighting and are quite elegant. There are different types of boudoir with garments and some with costumes or partially and wholly nude photos.

There is the pin up, the nude, the magazine and the in between boudoir. The pin up basically involves recreating a scene. It could be nude or seminude or with you in your lingerie. Then you create a scene that has drama. You could choose to do a burlesque look where you are looking like a burlesque dancer and this involves adding emotion and attitude to your poses. You can also recreate famous actresses' scenes. Then you can have a pose like Marilyn Monroe on set. The background is usually made to a certain setting it could be an old movie set or a black and white set to an old Hollywood look. One lady who had a boudoir photo shoot says it helped her regain her life. Claire Benet had a rough year after suffering a miscarriage after another. She felt devastated and she decided to try the boudoir photo shoot and the results just made her yearn to live a full life once again.

The nude boudoir photo shoots usually require you to strip down but they can be taken in good angles so you don't come off looking trashy. The photographer can also suggest poses to you that do not show the parts of the body you don't want to reveal. You can use a sheet to slightly cover your body. The boudoir photographer is a professional and will make you feel as comfortable as possible while taking your pictures. You should always let the photographer know what you are comfortable with and what makes you uncomfortable.

The Magazine boudoir is done by people who want the photos to appear on magazines and they won't go for a full nude. This picture will just suggest a hint of nudism without actually showing you the person nude. It also focuses on the face as the person would want to be seen by the viewers. The hinted nudity increases the sensuality of the photograph. One celebrity who went for this shoot was Keira Knightley the famous actress in Pirates of the Caribbean went topless on the Interview Magazine and didn't even try to cover up she had her hands on her sides and the picture is done in good taste. Another celebrity who did the boudoir photo shoot for a magazine was also topless though she covered up using her hands. The way you want your photo done is what they will work with.

Then there is the sneak peek type of boudoir where you look like you are just about to strip down. This look is absolutely sexy and will have you looking like a ravishing goddess. The idea is to bring your own clothing items it could be a shirt and the photo will be captured with you taking off the shirt. It just really provides a sexy photo and piques the curiosity of anyone who would see it.

Don't worry you won't be caught unaware with leaked photos on the Internet to become like the break the Internet Star the socialite and business woman Kim Kardashian who did release her photos intentionally. While doing boudoir photos you will get to choose the best type for you and you can tell the photographer about your privacy needs. If you want the photos shared or if you want them discreetly done. Most of the boudoir photographers are quite professional and they won't release your private pictures to anyone without your consent.

You can decide to do all the styles and create an album showing you in all these types of boudoir.

Chapter 4: How To Prepare For Your First Boudoir Photography Shoot

When you decide to go for your first boudoir photo session you will need to be prepared. First set your mind on doing it then check online for boudoir photographers and their studios located around you. Then select one of the photographer's and commit to the photography taking place. The photos can be taken in any setting of your choice. You can have them come to your home if that is what you are comfortable with. Going to the studio for the photo shoot is much more preferable because you know they have everything they need there. Imagine if they forgot a piece of equipment that would enhance the photos during the shoot, some photographers won't go back and get what they need especially if they are highly booked. So prepare yourself to go there a little bit ahead than the set schedule. This will give you ample time to calm your nerves and get ready for the shoot.

Before the time for going to the actual shoot you should study various poses online. You can get some inspiration from instagram, pinterest and websites for boudoir to just see some poses you would like to try. While the photographer may direct you on the poses you should have some general ideas of the poses you want to take. Then you will have an easier time at the session.

Now what are you going to wear? While most boudoir photographers have sexy outfits you may want to get your own fit of sexy clothes. Get the best lingerie and sexy negligees that you can. You can pick sexy bras and underwear that have lace. Get a corset, some robes and if you want it to be a gift for your significant other you can carry their shirt to strike a sexy pose with it.

You definitely want to get your hair and makeup looking its best for the photos. Some photographers include makeup and hair in the package. Unless you want a particular type of hairstyle the studio will be equipped with makeup and hair accessories for your hair. One of the new things you may notice with the makeup is most photographers want to add fake eye lashes to just bring out your eyes more. You shouldn't worry too much about this they won't get the very long dramatic lashes. You may think the makeup is too much but the photographer has already considered this and has made the necessary adjustments to the light and camera so that it looks just right.

The first part is usually hair and makeup and this can take one hour or more and you should keep well hydrated before the photo shoot because some of the poses may require you to remain in the position while the photographer selects the right angle to take the photo.

The whole thing can last from 1 and a half hours to longer and you don't have to worry about the poses as they will let you know which poses are the most sexy and bring out your best features. Then you should let them know if you want to bring someone along and usually the shoot will only have to people in the room so you don't have to feel embarrassed about people seeing you in your underwear.

Chapter 5: Poses for your Boudoir shoot

One of the poses you can try is lying on your back, eyes looking at the camera and your body is seen on the background with the lingerie of your choice. If you want to get a full body pose with the whole body being seen try and make half turn and then stand with your heels on. The heels will help elongate your sexy legs.

Then you can lie on your stomach with your head facing the camera and the rest of your body being seen in the background. Propping your arms can help bring your breasts into the picture and raising your bottom will also allow it to be in the picture. Another way to do this pose is to not let your stomach touch the bed or covers but instead pose in a half crawl and the picture can be taken from the side of your body.

Then you can kneel in front of the camera and have your legs spread wide in the photo in your sexy underwear. For a magazine pose you can remove the bra and have a robe covering the top of your body and sexy underwear. Leave the robe half open and give a glimpse of your breasts. This is a sensual pose that will have you looking like the sexy vixen you are.

For the nude and seminude poses you can cover your breasts and vagina using your hands and legs. You can have one leg on top of the other to just cover up. You can also tilt your body where you are on the bed and you lean on one side and cover up with a sheet to create an illusion of being fully nude.

Some of the other moves you may want to try are the classic look where you can imitate famous poses that were done in history. Lewis Morley's picture is one way to do a full nude without showing your entire body. The pose captured in 1963 has her seated on a chair backwards holding the chair only her legs and shoulders can be seen in this nude boudoir. Then you can do a nude without props by just raising your leg and leaning on your thigh to cover up your body. You can also trying burlesque posing which can have you wearing sexy underwear and heels. The makeup is thick and shows a dancer in heels. You can do a full nude with feathers covering your body and a headgear to further the costume. Then you can change the venue of the shoot you can do it outside in the natural light and still look tasteful.

Then you can try a number of poses that would seem interesting to you. You can use the poses above as a guideline and add your own little twist. To be a better natural at the posing of the pictures you can practice the moves often in your house before the shoot. Don't try and suck in your stomach or go on a crash diet so that you look slimmer at the photo shoot. The pictures are meant to be a reflection of who you really are and an adoration of how sexy you look in your current state.

For the classical look you can tell the photographer whether you would prefer the photos in black and white or for them to have color before the shoot. For all the photos actually you can decide to do a black and white theme. To be more dramatic you could wear brightly colored lingerie and get the photographer to show the bright color of the lingerie in the black and white background. As you read this you will find that you are coming up with several sexy ideas to add to your photos and you will want to add them to the shoot. You can even add small aspects about yourself like whether you are a cook the theme can be based on a kitchen or if you love to work hard you can create the illusion of being in the office with just a white office wear shirt.

Refer to the very last page of this book to see some examples of enticing boudoir poses, techniques and angles. You can also just do a simple Google search for "Boudoir Poses" to get a few ideas for some sexy angles and poses!

Chapter 6: Tips for Successful Boudoir Photography

As seen in the previous chapters boudoir photography is something you want to do to feel sexy and confident about yourself. There are a few tricks that you can do during your photo shoot to create more artistic and sexy poses.

First try and identify the parts of yourself that you love the most. The parts of your body that are the most stunning should be in poses with those features being prominent in the photographs. Any part of your body that you like the most you can create poses that focus on those parts.

Then don't look at the camera directly, try and make the photos look suggestive by closing your eyes or looking aside. Then after a few photos you can look at the camera directly with a particular attitude. It just helps you ease into the photo shoot and be more confident.

There's the way you should work towards the main light to avoid having shadowy photographs. You can try posing in different angles to find the best natural light. To do this you should ask to see the photos even as the shoot is going on.

Then change your expression in the different photos according to how you feel and you can just be able to convey a lot of confidence as you do so. For the nudes or if you are going totally nude you should arch your back, keep your toes pointed and just keep the shoes off. When you are in sexy underwear or a sexy robe then you can have the heels on.

You can have different themes for your boudoir photography depending on your likes and what you are going through in that particular stage of your life. Women are starting to do bridal themed boudoir photography to gift to their husbands to be or husbands. One of the ways to make it bridal is to select white lingerie and do get the photos taken in a white background. This will create a wedding theme for the photos. Then you can have a veil you can wear it with the lingerie even as you make the poses for the boudoir photography. To add a wedding vibe to the whole shoot you can have some wine glasses, a champagne bottle and even a bouquet of flowers. You can even do a nude pose with only the veil covering your body as you lie down. Or you can kneel and hold a glass of champagne or have the glasses and champagne in a corner.

If you are into sports and would like a more sports related sort of boudoir an outside pool photo shoot is a great way to create this look. Make sure the sun does not ruin your look or picture pose. Then you can either get into the pool or by the side of it. Another look you can try indoors is using a racket. You can sit in the nude and have the racket cover your body. You can use various sport items as a prop. You can start with soccer balls, a gym locker background or even some basketballs.

The Burlesque theme is a sexy way to showcase your body. You should imagine yourself as a sexy dancer and be able to exude that sort of attitude. The costumes for burlesque dancers are endless and include corsets, sexy lingerie, panty hoses and sexy stockings. You should be ready to wear these sexy clothes. Then there is a lot of drama in the setting with the theme colors being bright and the photos using side lighting to just capture the color theme of the photograph. You can change your hair for this theme or you can use a wig. Then there are a lot of mirrors in some of the themes that just enhance the theme.

You can consider using mirror for your boudoir photos. They can help you go through it without feeling shy as the images on the mirror are sort of in the background. They can also help you enhance your theme through focusing on specific parts of the room.

The photographer can also be approached if you want to hide certain scars or if you want the photos retouched to remove stretch marks and cellulite.

If you don't feel comfortable going nude you really don't have to. You can select nude lingerie or clothes that just look nude and do the photo shoot.

Following all these tips will help you get ready for your first photo shoot so you don't feel lost once you get there. There are other themes you can look for to try out. You can try the movie themes where you can use scenes you have watched from a particular movie to help you form the basis of your photos.

Conclusion:

Taking boudoir photos is something you can get done with ease. Any woman can take boudoir photos despite their age, shape or size. This is an art form that is suitable for all women. You can find a good photographer and check their previous work to help pick the most suitable style for you. Thank you for getting this book and I hope the tips and knowledge here will help you get through several successful boudoir photo shoots. You can always start with some simple poses and move to more complex ones. Then you get to choose the location to somewhere you can be comfortable in. The photographers are professional and because they want you to tell your friends about it they will keep your privacy and will be quite encouraging throughout the whole shoot. You won't have to go through tons of books to get ready. In this book we have shown you how to best prepare for the photo session.

You have also learned several poses that you can try out and start looking like the sexy woman that you really are. These photos will leave you feeling confident and help you try all the things that you want to without looking at being a woman as a hindrance.

You have seen the various types of women who tried taking the photos and how good they felt about themselves afterwards. It shouldn't matter where you are in your life whether you are young, you are pregnant (Kourtney Kardashian took some great boudoir photos while being pregnant), you have a terminal disease or you are going through a bad time in your life these photos will help give you hope to achieve anything you set yourself to do.

Enjoy your boudoir photos and I hope you keep taking more and more photos to see how sexy you can be!

Thank you again for downloading this book! I hope it was able to provide you genuine value!

Finally, if you enjoyed this book and believe that it can serve and provide value to others, please leave feedback to help promote and support our goal of helping more and more readers! Afterwards please take a moment to check out my other books as well as join my Publishing Partners Free Newsletter for Free Bonus Content! (Details on following pages.)

Flip past the final page of this book to leave a review on Amazon!

Thank you and good luck!

Check Out My Publishing Partners Books & Join Her Free Newsletter!

Amazon: www.amazon.com/author/cassandraslain

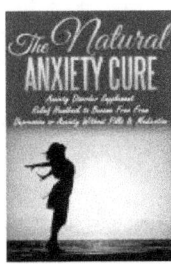**Natural Anxiety Cure:** http://amzn.to/1Jx86Zl

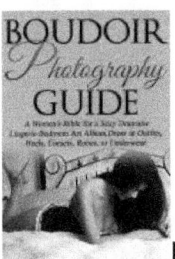**Boudoir Photography Guide:** http://amzn.to/1AUynOl

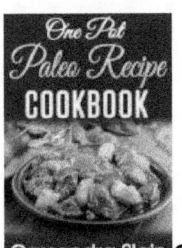**One Pot Paleo Recipe Cookbook:** http://amzn.to/1dWBgo1

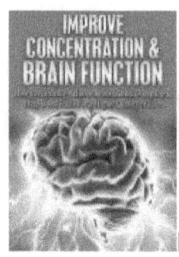**Improve Concentration & Brain Function:**

http://amzn.to/1QCyMXM

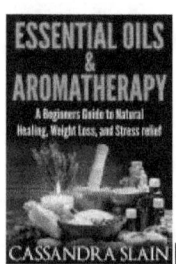Essential Oils & Aromatherapy: http://amzn.to/1KZpWES

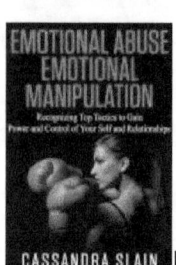Emotional   Abuse   &   Emotional   Manipulation:

http://amzn.to/1Kn5woj

Join   Cassandras   Free   Newsletter!:http://eepurl.com/bpHpdH

Here are just a few pictures of some sexy poses. You can also just do a simple Google search for "Boudoir Poses" to get infinite ideas for some sexy angles and poses!

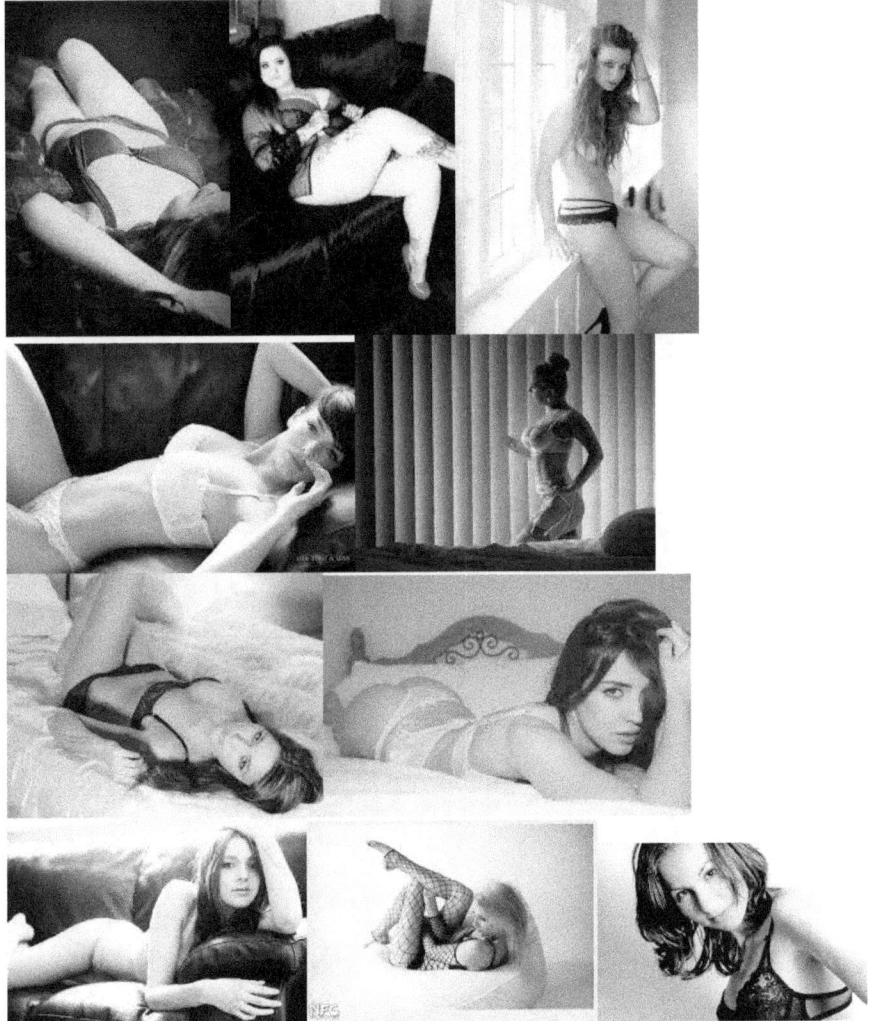

www.ingramcontent.com/pod-product-compliance
Lightning Source LLC
Chambersburg PA
CBHW070801180526
45168CB00004B/1713